The Sovereign Individual, Made Simple

Praise for Hugo Thornton Rowley

Just brilliant. Learner's Permit Guides make dense topics accessible.

— Philip von Dirksen

Solid reference guide for technocrats and wannabes alike. Love reading something that makes me question if its written for billionaires, Antifa or just bog-standard Libertarians.

— Janice Good

Rowley brings "The Sovereign Individual" to life.

— Will Stephenson

The Sovereign Individual, Made Simple

A Learner's Permit for the Collapse of the Welfare State and the Rise of the Information Age

Learner's Permit Guides

Hugo Thornton Rowley

Kid Sister Books

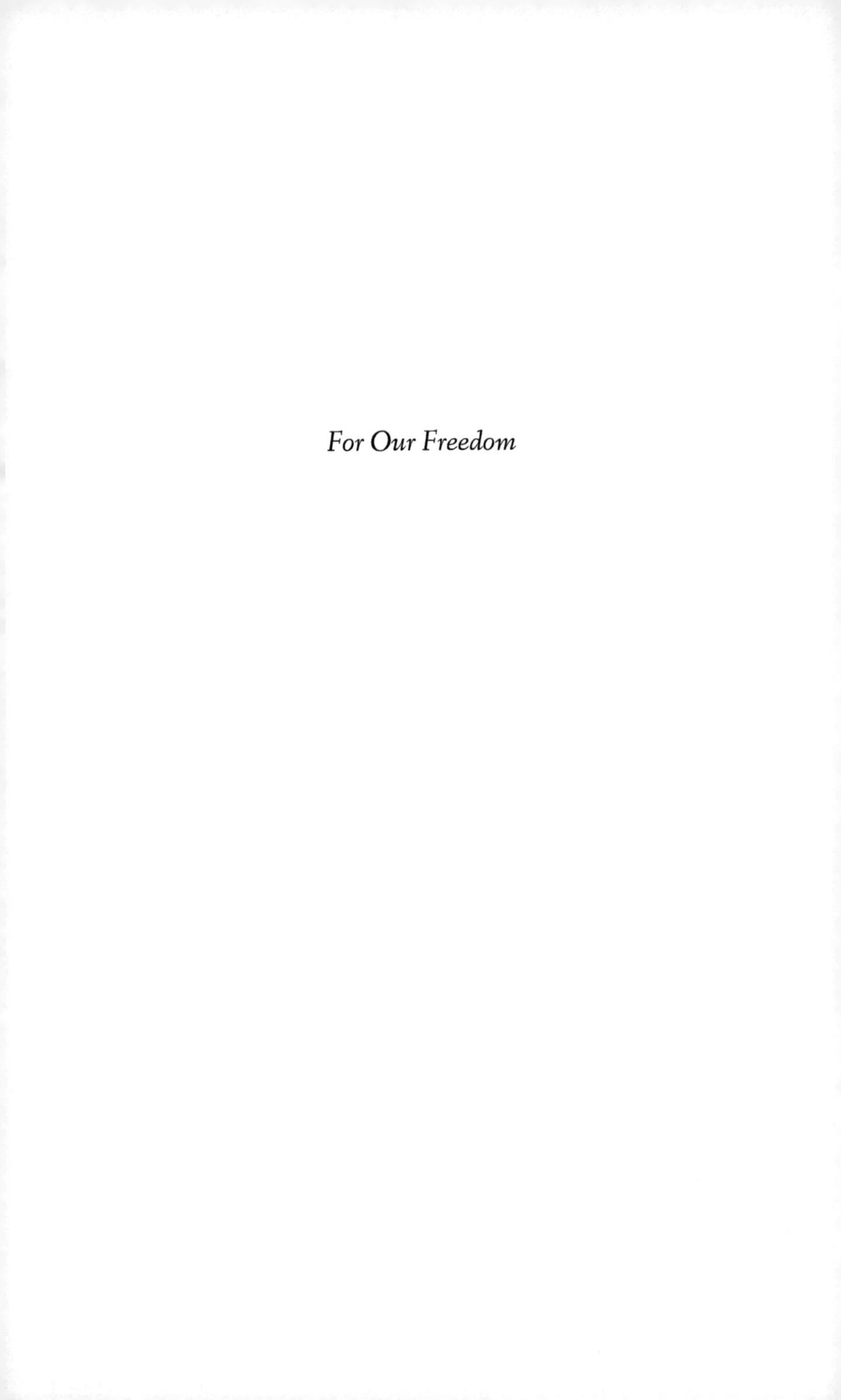

For Our Freedom

Man is born free, but everywhere he is in chains.

— Jean-Jacques Rousseau

Introduction

Think of this book as your crib notes for the core philosophy informing key business and political figures in the 21st Century some even describe it as The Technocrat's Bible.

"The Sovereign Individual: Mastering the Transition to the Information Age" was written by James Dale Davidson and William Rees-Mogg and published in 1997; the work has turned out to be incredibly forward-thinking, predicting many of the huge changes we've seen as the Information Age has taken over.

"The Sovereign Individual" argues that the impact of the Information Revolution will be just as massive as the Agricultural and Industrial Revolutions were. These earlier revolutions drastically changed the balance of power between people and institutions, and the Information Age is set to do the same. According to Davidson and Rees-Mogg, this shift will give individuals more power and autonomy than ever before.

One of the book's big ideas is that the nation-state will lose its grip as the main form of social and political organization. With information technology making it harder for states to control and regulate economies, power will move from central governments to decentralized networks and markets. This means people will have more freedom to shape their own lives without being limited by geography, nationality, or social class.

But it's not all smooth sailing. The rise of the "Sovereign Individual" brings new challenges and opportunities. We'll see new kinds of social and economic setups, like private cities, virtual communities, reputation markets, and digital currencies. To navigate this new world, we need to develop new skills like digital literacy, cross-cultural communication, entrepreneurship, and self-reliance.

This study guide is here to help you dive into the book's key ideas and arguments. It provides a framework for thinking about and discussing these concepts.

In the following chapters, we'll cover the major themes and ideas in "The Sovereign Individual," including the decline of the nation-state, the rise of private law, and the commercialization of sovereignty. We'll also introduce important vocabulary and give practical tips on how you can apply these ideas in your own life and career.

Whether you're an entrepreneur, an investor, a policymaker, or just curious about how our world is changing, "The Sovereign Individual" has a lot to offer. By understanding the Information Revolution and developing the skills to thrive in this new era, you can position yourself to succeed as a Sovereign Individual.

So let's get started on this journey of discovery and transformation. Together, we'll explore the challenges and opportunities of the Information Age and work towards a future of greater freedom, prosperity, and individual empowerment.

Key Ideas:

• Nation-states will lose power as individuals gain the ability to operate globally without borders.

• A "cognitive elite" will gain massive wealth and influence.

• The rise of independent economic agents will result in greater inequality.

• Traditional concepts like citizenship and democracy will be challenged.

• The depth of changes will transform all aspects of modern society.

Vocabulary:

• Sovereign Individual: Individuals who can operate independently of nation-states due to their ability to earn high incomes in the global economy and protect their wealth through technology.

• Megapolitics: The study of the hidden causes of social and political change, focusing on factors that alter the logic of violence.

• Cognitive Elite: A group of highly skilled and

educated individuals who will gain disproportionate wealth and influence in the Information Age.

Practical Applications:

• Consider how the changing global landscape may affect your career, investments, and lifestyle choices.

• Develop skills and knowledge that will be valuable in the Information Age economy.

• Be prepared for potential social and political upheaval as traditional institutions and concepts are challenged.

Chapter 1

The Transition of the Year 2000 - The Fourth Stage of Human Society

The stage is set for an exploration of the profound changes that the Information Age will bring to human society. The transition from the Industrial Age to the Information Age represents the fourth major stage in human societal development, following the hunting-and-gathering, agricultural, and industrial stages.

A sense of unease and anticipation surrounded the approach of the year 2000, with many people feeling that the world was on the brink of significant change. The Information Revolution will have far-reaching consequences, transforming every aspect of society and leading to the rise of the "Sovereign Individual."

There are parallels between the current situation and previous transformative periods in history, such as the end of the 15th century, when the medieval Church was losing its power and influence. Just as the shift from the medieval world to the modern era brought about profound changes in society, politics, and economics, so too will the transition from the Industrial Age to the Information Age.

The Information Revolution will lead to a significant redistribution of power and wealth, with a "cognitive elite" of highly skilled and adaptable individuals benefiting disproportionately from the new technologies and economic arrangements. Returns to large-scale violence will decrease, leading to a rise in crime and a decline in the power of nation-states as their monopoly on violence erodes.

The pace and global impact of the Information Revolution will be unprecedented, with the potential for rapid and widespread changes in society and the economy.

Key Ideas:

- The Information Revolution represents the fourth stage of human societal development, following the hunting-and-gathering, agricultural, and industrial stages.
- The transition from the Industrial Age to the Information Age will have profound consequences, transforming every aspect of society and leading to the rise of the "Sovereign Individual."
- The current period of change is similar to previous transformative moments in history,

such as the end of the medieval era and the beginning of the modern age.
- The Information Revolution will lead to a redistribution of power and wealth, with a "cognitive elite" benefiting disproportionately from the new technologies and economic arrangements.
- The returns to large-scale violence will decrease, leading to a rise in crime and a decline in the power of nation-states as their monopoly on violence erodes.
- The pace and global impact of the Information Revolution will be unprecedented.

Vocabulary:

1. Industrial Age: The period of human history characterized by the rise of industrial production, mass manufacturing, and the factory system, typically dated from the mid-18th century to the mid-20th century.
2. Information Age: The period of human history characterized by the rise of digital technologies, the internet, and the knowledge economy, typically dated from the late 20th century to the present.

3. Sovereign Individual: The type of individual who will thrive in the Information Age highly skilled, adaptable, and able to operate independently of traditional institutions and structures.
4. Cognitive Elite: The group of individuals who will benefit disproportionately from the Information Revolution, due to their high levels of skill, knowledge, and creativity.
5. Microtechnology: The branch of technology that deals with the miniaturization of electronic components and devices, enabling the development of increasingly powerful and portable computing and communication technologies.
6. Information Society: A society characterized by the central role of information and communication technologies in economic, social, and political life.
7. Monopoly on Violence: The concept that the state holds the exclusive right to use or authorize the use of physical force within its territory.
8. Hydraulic Civilizations: Ancient civilizations that relied on centralized control of water resources, such as those in Egypt and Mesopotamia.

Practical Applications:

1. Embrace lifelong learning: To thrive in the Information Age, individuals will need to continually update their skills and knowledge to keep pace with rapid technological and economic change. This means embracing a mindset of lifelong learning and being proactive about seeking out new opportunities for growth and development.

2. Develop a global mindset: As the Information Revolution erodes the significance of geographic boundaries, individuals who are able to think and operate globally will be better positioned to take advantage of new opportunities. This means cultivating cross-cultural awareness, learning new languages, and building networks and relationships that span multiple countries and regions.

3. Build resilience and adaptability: The Information Age will be characterized by rapid change and disruption, with many traditional industries and job roles becoming obsolete. To navigate this uncertainty, individuals will need to cultivate resilience and adaptability, being open to new experiences and willing to pivot in response to changing circumstances.

. . .

4. Cultivate a strong personal brand: In a world where traditional institutions and credentials are losing their relevance, individuals will need to take greater responsibility for marketing themselves and their unique value proposition. This means developing a strong personal brand, leveraging online platforms and networks to showcase one's skills and accomplishments, and building a reputation as a thought leader and expert in one's field.

5. Embrace entrepreneurship and self-employment: As the traditional job market becomes more precarious and unpredictable, many individuals will need to create their own opportunities by starting businesses or working as freelancers and consultants. This means developing an entrepreneurial mindset, being proactive about identifying and pursuing new opportunities, and building a diverse portfolio of skills and revenue streams.

6. Assess your skills and knowledge in light of the changing economic landscape of the Information Age.

7. Consider the potential implications of decreased returns to large-scale violence for personal safety and security.

. . .

8. Be aware of the potential for rapid and widespread changes in society and the economy due to the Information Revolution.

Chapter 2

The Megapolitics of the Information Age - The Triumph of Efficiency over Power Summary

Megapolitics are the interactions between politics, technology, and society. The Information Age will bring about a fundamental shift in the balance of power between individuals and institutions, as the increasing efficiency and accessibility of information undermines traditional sources of authority and control.

The nation-state, which has been the dominant form of political organization in the modern era, is particularly vulnerable to the disruptive effects of the Information Revolution. As the global economy becomes increasingly interconnected and decentralized, the ability of nation-states to control and regulate economic activity within their borders will be severely diminished. At the same time, the rise of digital technologies and networked communication will make it easier for individuals and non-state actors to organize and coordinate their activities across borders, challenging the monopoly on power and legitimacy that nation-states have historically enjoyed.

These trends will lead to a "triumph of efficiency over power," as the traditional institutions of the Industrial Age give way to more fluid and adaptable forms of social and economic organization. The key to success in the Information Age will be the ability to leverage technology and information to create value and solve problems, rather than relying on the coercive power of the state or other centralized authorities.

Several key factors that will contribute to the decline of nation-state power, including microtechnology and rapidly falling information costs, which will undermine the state's ability to tax and regulate economic activity. The increasing importance of cyberspace as a realm of economic and social activity that transcends geographic boundaries and operates beyond the reach of territorial governments.

Ultimately, the nation-state will face a crisis of legitimacy as its ability to provide services and security declines, paving the way for a new era of individual autonomy and entrepreneurship.

Key Ideas:

- The Information Age will bring about a fundamental shift in the balance of power between individuals and institutions, as the increasing efficiency and accessibility of information undermines traditional sources of authority and control.

- The nation-state is particularly vulnerable to the disruptive effects of the Information Revolution, as its ability to control and regulate economic activity within its borders is diminished by the rise of the global, networked economy.
- The rise of digital technologies and networked communication will make it easier for individuals and non-state actors to organize and coordinate their activities across borders, challenging the monopoly on power and legitimacy that nation-states have historically enjoyed.
- Microtechnology and rapidly falling information costs will undermine the power of nation-states to tax and regulate economic activity.
- Individuals and businesses will increasingly operate in cyberspace, beyond the reach of territorial governments.
- The nation-state will face a crisis of legitimacy as its ability to provide services and security declines.
- The key to success in the Information Age will be the ability to leverage technology and information to create value and solve problems, rather than relying on the coercive

power of the state or other centralized authorities.

Vocabulary:

1. Megapolitics: The study of the interactions between politics, technology, and society, particularly as they relate to the distribution and exercise of power.
2. Information Revolution: The rapid and transformative changes in the way that information is created, distributed, and consumed, driven by the rise of digital technologies and the internet.
3. Decentralization: The process by which power and decision-making authority is distributed away from a central point of control and towards a more diffuse network of actors and institutions.
4. Non-State Actors: Individuals, groups, and organizations that operate independently of the state and its institutions, such as corporations, NGOs, and international organizations.
5. Networked Economy: An economy characterized by the increasing interconnectedness and interdependence of economic actors and activities, facilitated by

digital technologies and global communication networks.
6. Microtechnology: Technologies that enable the miniaturization and personalization of devices and systems, such as microprocessors and nanotechnology.
7. Cyberspace: The virtual realm of computer networks and digital communication, which transcends geographic boundaries.
8. Jurisdictional Arbitrage: The practice of choosing the most favorable legal or regulatory environment for one's activities, often by operating across multiple jurisdictions.

Practical Applications:

1. Develop digital literacy and technological skills: To thrive in the Information Age, individuals will need to be comfortable with and proficient in the use of digital technologies and tools. This means investing in ongoing education and training to stay up-to-date with the latest developments in areas such as data analysis, programming, and cybersecurity.

2. Cultivate a network mindset: In a world where power and influence are increasingly decentralized and distributed, individuals who are able to build and

leverage networks will be better positioned to succeed. This means cultivating relationships and partnerships across different sectors and geographies, and being open to collaboration and resource-sharing.

3. Embrace innovation and experimentation: The Information Age will be characterized by rapid change and disruption, with many traditional business models and ways of working becoming obsolete. To stay ahead of the curve, individuals and organizations will need to embrace a culture of innovation and experimentation, being willing to take risks and try new approaches in order to create value and solve problems.

4. Develop a global perspective: As the world becomes increasingly interconnected and interdependent, individuals who are able to think and operate on a global scale will be better positioned to take advantage of new opportunities. This means cultivating cross-cultural awareness and understanding, building relationships with partners and collaborators around the world, and being open to new ideas and perspectives.

5. Focus on creating value and solving problems: In the Information Age, the most successful individuals and organizations will be those that are able to leverage technology and information to create value and solve real-

world problems. This means shifting away from a focus on accumulating power and control, and towards a more entrepreneurial and solutions-oriented mindset.

6. Consider how the decline of nation-state power may affect your personal and business activities.

7. Explore opportunities to leverage microtechnology and cyberspace to operate more efficiently and independently.

8. Be prepared for potential disruptions in government services and security as the nation-state faces a crisis of legitimacy.

Chapter 3

Transcending Locality - The Emergence of the Cybereconomy

The concept of the "cybereconomy" is the emerging global economic system that is based on the creation, exchange, and consumption of digital goods and services. The rise of the cybereconomy represents a fundamental shift in the way that economic activity is organized and conducted, with far-reaching implications for individuals, businesses, and societies around the world.

One of the key features of the cybereconomy is its ability to transcend traditional geographic and political boundaries. Unlike the physical economy of the Industrial Age, which was largely constrained by the limitations of transportation and communication technologies, the cybereconomy operates in a virtual space that is accessible from anywhere in the world with an internet connection. This means that individuals and businesses can participate in the global economy regardless of their physical location, opening up new opportunities for trade, collaboration, and innovation.

The rise of the cybereconomy will allow individuals and businesses to operate globally without being tied to any specific location. The development of digital currencies, smart contracts, and other decentralized technologies will enable individuals to conduct transactions and exchange value without the need for intermediaries or centralized authorities. This will lead to the cybereconomy becoming the largest and most important economic realm, transcending geographic boundaries.

Digital money and encryption will play a crucial role in the cybereconomy, enabling individuals to protect their wealth and conduct transactions without government interference. The rise of the cybereconomy will also lead to increased competition among jurisdictions to attract wealth and talent, as the traditional power of nation-states to control economic activity within their borders diminishes.

This will also pose significant challenges and risks. The increasing digitization of economic activity will lead to the displacement of many traditional jobs and industries, as automation and artificial intelligence render many forms of human labor obsolete. The cybereconomy will be characterized by increasing returns to scale and network effects, leading to the concentration of wealth and power in the hands of a small number of dominant platforms and ecosystems.

To navigate these challenges and opportunities, individuals and organizations will need to develop new skills and strategies for creating value in the cybereconomy. This will involve leveraging digital technologies and data to create innovative products and services, building and cultivating online communities and networks, and developing new business models and revenue streams that are not dependent on traditional forms of economic exchange.

Key Ideas:

- The rise of the cybereconomy represents a fundamental shift in the way that economic activity is organized and conducted, with far-reaching implications for individuals, businesses, and societies around the world.
- The cybereconomy operates in a virtual space that is accessible from anywhere in the world with an internet connection, transcending traditional geographic and political boundaries.
- The cybereconomy will become the largest and most important economic realm, transcending geographic boundaries.
- Digital money and encryption will enable individuals to protect their wealth and conduct transactions without government interference.

- The rise of the cybereconomy will lead to increased competition among jurisdictions to attract wealth and talent.
- The increasing digitization of economic activity will lead to the displacement of many traditional jobs and industries, as automation and artificial intelligence render many forms of human labor obsolete.
- The cybereconomy will be characterized by increasing returns to scale and network effects, leading to the concentration of wealth and power in the hands of a small number of dominant platforms and ecosystems.
- To thrive in the cybereconomy, individuals and organizations will need to develop new skills and strategies for creating value, leveraging digital technologies and data, building online communities and networks, and developing new business models and revenue streams.

Vocabulary:

1. Cybereconomy: The emerging global economic system that is based on the creation, exchange, and consumption of digital goods and services.

2. Digital Goods and Services: Products and services that are created, delivered, and consumed in a digital format, such as software, online content, and cloud-based services.
3. Digital Money: Electronic forms of currency that can be used for online transactions and stored securely using cryptography.
4. Encryption: The process of encoding information to protect it from unauthorized access or tampering.
5. Increasing Returns to Scale: The economic phenomenon whereby the cost of producing each additional unit of a good or service decreases as the scale of production increases, leading to a competitive advantage for larger firms and platforms.
6. Network Effects: The phenomenon whereby the value of a product or service increases as more people use it, creating a self-reinforcing cycle of growth and adoption.
7. Platform Economy: An economic system characterized by the dominance of digital platforms that facilitate interactions and transactions between multiple groups of users, such as consumers, producers, and advertisers.

Practical Applications:

1. Develop digital skills and capabilities: To participate effectively in the cybereconomy, individuals will need to develop a range of digital skills and capabilities, such as data analysis, programming, and digital marketing. This may involve pursuing formal education and training in these areas, as well as engaging in ongoing self-directed learning and experimentation.

2. Embrace remote work and digital collaboration: The cybereconomy enables individuals to work and collaborate with others regardless of their physical location, opening up new opportunities for flexibility and mobility in employment. To take advantage of these opportunities, individuals will need to develop effective strategies for remote work and digital collaboration, such as using online communication and project management tools, and building strong relationships with colleagues and partners.

3. Leverage data and analytics: In the cybereconomy, data is a key source of value and competitive advantage. Individuals and organizations that are able to collect, analyze, and utilize data effectively will be better positioned to make informed decisions, develop targeted products and services, and optimize their operations and processes.

. . .

4. Build and cultivate online communities: The cybereconomy is characterized by the increasing importance of online communities and networks, which can serve as powerful platforms for marketing, customer engagement, and innovation. To succeed in this environment, individuals and organizations will need to develop effective strategies for building and cultivating online communities, such as creating compelling content, fostering meaningful interactions and relationships, and leveraging social media and other digital channels.

5. Experiment with new business models and revenue streams: The cybereconomy is disrupting traditional business models and creating new opportunities for value creation and capture. To thrive in this environment, individuals and organizations will need to be open to experimentation and innovation, exploring new ways of generating revenue and creating value for customers and stakeholders. This may involve developing new products and services, leveraging digital platforms and marketplaces, or exploring alternative financing and ownership models.

6. Familiarize yourself with digital technologies and virtual business models to take advantage of opportunities in the cybereconomy.

. . .

7. Consider using digital money and encryption to protect your financial assets and transactions from government interference.

8. Be aware of the potential for increased competition among jurisdictions and consider how this may affect your personal and business decisions.

Chapter 4

The End of Egalitarian Economics - The Revolution in Earnings Capacity in a World Without Jobs

There are profound implications in the Information Age for the nature of work, income, and wealth distribution. The rise of digital technologies and the cybereconomy will lead to a fundamental shift in the way that economic rewards are allocated, with far-reaching consequences for social and political stability.

One of the key features of the Information Age will be the increasing importance of human capital and cognitive skills as drivers of economic value creation. As machines and algorithms take over many routine and repetitive tasks, the demand for workers with *specialized knowledge, creativity, and problem-solving* abilities will increase, leading to a growing premium on education and talent.

At the same time, however, the Information Age will also be characterized by a significant decline in the overall demand for human labor, as automation and artificial intelligence render many traditional jobs and occupations obsolete. This will lead to a growing polarization of the workforce, with a small number of highly skilled and well-compensated "knowledge workers" at one end of the spectrum, and a large number of low-skilled and precarious service workers at the other.

Those with exceptional skills and creativity will be rewarded, leading to a "winner-take-all" economy. Many traditional jobs will disappear as automation and artificial intelligence replace human labor, and the concept of a "job" as a long-term, full-time employment relationship will become obsolete.

This polarization will have profound implications for social and political stability, as the traditional mechanisms of income redistribution and social welfare become increasingly strained. The Information Age will require a fundamental rethinking of the social contract, with new forms of income and wealth distribution that are not tied to traditional employment relationships.

To navigate these challenges, individuals and societies will need to embrace a more entrepreneurial and adaptive approach to work and income generation. This will involve developing new skills and capabilities that are aligned with the demands of the cybereconomy, as well as exploring alternative forms of employment and income generation, such as freelancing, consulting, and digital entrepreneurship.

Key Ideas:

- The Information Age will lead to a fundamental shift in the way that economic rewards are allocated, with a growing premium on human capital and cognitive skills as drivers of value creation.
- The rise of automation and artificial intelligence will lead to a significant decline in the overall demand for human labor, rendering many traditional jobs and occupations obsolete.
- The Information Age will reward those with exceptional skills and creativity, leading to a "winner-take-all" economy.
- Many traditional jobs will disappear as automation and artificial intelligence replace human labor, and the concept of a "job" as a long-term, full-time employment relationship will become obsolete.
- The workforce will become increasingly polarized, with a small number of highly skilled and well-compensated "knowledge workers" at one end of the spectrum, and a large number of low-skilled and precarious service workers at the other.
- The traditional mechanisms of income redistribution and social welfare will become increasingly strained, requiring a fundamental rethinking of the social contract and new forms of income and wealth distribution.

- To thrive in the Information Age, individuals and societies will need to embrace a more entrepreneurial and adaptive approach to work and income generation, developing new skills and exploring alternative forms of employment and income generation.

Vocabulary:

1. Human Capital: The knowledge, skills, and abilities that individuals possess, and that contribute to their economic productivity and value creation potential.
2. Cognitive Skills: The mental processes and abilities that enable individuals to acquire, process, and apply knowledge, such as problem-solving, critical thinking, and creativity.
3. Knowledge Workers: Individuals whose primary value contribution comes from their ability to create, analyze, and apply knowledge and information, rather than from their physical labor or manual skills.
4. Precariat: A social class characterized by precarious and insecure employment, low wages, and limited access to social benefits and protections.

5. Digital Entrepreneurship: The practice of creating and running a business that is primarily based on digital technologies and the internet, often with a focus on innovation, scalability, and global reach.
6. Winner-Take-All Economy: An economic system in which a small number of top performers capture a disproportionate share of rewards.
7. Skill Premium: The additional compensation that highly skilled workers earn compared to less-skilled workers.
8. Gig Economy: A labor market characterized by short-term contracts, freelance work, and independent contracting rather than permanent jobs.

Practical Applications:

1. Invest in continuous learning and skill development: To remain competitive in the Information Age, individuals will need to commit to ongoing learning and skill development throughout their careers. This may involve pursuing formal education and training programs, as well as engaging in self-directed learning and experimentation to stay up-to-date with emerging technologies and trends.

. . .

2. Develop a diverse portfolio of income streams: As traditional employment relationships become less stable and reliable, individuals will need to explore alternative forms of income generation and wealth creation. This may involve developing a portfolio of freelance or consulting work, investing in digital assets or platforms, or starting a business or side hustle.

3. Cultivate entrepreneurial skills and mindsets: The Information Age will reward individuals who are able to identify and pursue new opportunities for value creation and innovation. To succeed in this environment, individuals will need to cultivate entrepreneurial skills and mindsets, such as creativity, adaptability, risk-taking, and resilience.

4. Build a strong personal brand and network: In a world where traditional career paths and job security are declining, individuals will need to take a more proactive approach to managing their professional reputation and relationships. This may involve building a strong personal brand and online presence, as well as cultivating a diverse network of contacts and collaborators across different industries and geographies.

5. Advocate for new forms of social protection and wealth distribution: As the traditional social contract becomes

increasingly strained, individuals and societies will need to explore new forms of social protection and wealth distribution that are better aligned with the realities of the Information Age. This may involve advocating for policies such as universal basic income, portable benefits, or digital asset ownership, as well as exploring alternative models of governance and collective action.

6. Develop high-value skills and cultivate creativity to thrive in the winner-take-all economy.

7. Be prepared for the possibility of frequent job changes and periods of self-employment or freelance work.

8. Consider how the gig economy may affect your personal financial planning and career strategies.

Chapter 5

Nationalism, Reaction, and the New Luddites

There is potential for backlash against the transformative changes brought about by the Information Age. The rapid technological advancements and the consequent disruptions to traditional ways of life could give rise to a reactionary movement that seeks to maintain the status quo. This backlash could manifest in various forms, including the resurgence of nationalist sentiments, populist uprisings, and neo-Luddite resistance to automation and digitization.

One of the primary drivers of this backlash will be the widening gap between the beneficiaries of the Information Age and those left behind. As the rewards of the cybereconomy concentrate in the hands of a small, highly skilled elite, large segments of the population may face job insecurity, wage stagnation, and declining living standards. This growing inequality and polarization of wealth and income could fuel social and political unrest, as those who feel marginalized and disenfranchised by technological change seek to protect their interests and way of life.

This discontent could lead to the rise of nationalist and populist movements that aim to reassert the primacy of the nation-state and defend the interests of "ordinary" citizens against the perceived threats of globalization and technological disruption. These movements could advocate for protectionist trade policies, stricter border controls, and the rejection of international institutions and agreements that are seen as undermining national sovereignty and identity.

There is the possibility of a neo-Luddite resistance to the automation and digitization of the workforce. As machines and algorithms increasingly replace human labor across industries, some individuals and groups may resort to sabotage or violence to protect their livelihoods and resist the erosion of traditional employment structures.

To navigate these challenges, individuals and societies must find ways to balance the benefits of technological progress with the need for social and political stability. This may involve developing new forms of social protection and wealth distribution to mitigate the disruptive effects of the Information Age, as well as investing in education and training programs that enable individuals to adapt to the changing demands of the cybereconomy. Ultimately, fostering a culture of lifelong learning, adaptability, and responsible innovation will be crucial in navigating the complex landscape of the Information Age.

. . .

Key Ideas:

- The rapid technological changes of the Information Age could trigger a reactionary backlash from those seeking to preserve the status quo.
- Growing inequality and polarization of wealth and income may fuel nationalist and populist movements that aim to protect the interests of those left behind by technological disruption.
- Neo-Luddite resistance to automation and digitization could emerge as individuals and groups seek to protect their livelihoods and traditional employment structures.
- Balancing the benefits of technological progress with the need for social and political stability will be crucial in navigating the challenges of the Information Age.
- Developing new forms of social protection, promoting education and training, and fostering a culture of adaptability and responsible innovation will be key strategies for individuals and societies to thrive in the face of technological change.

Vocabulary:

1. Cybereconomy: The economic system that emerges as a result of the widespread adoption of digital technologies and the Internet, characterized by the increasing importance of information, knowledge, and digital assets.
2. Globalization: The process by which businesses, technologies, and philosophies spread throughout the world, leading to increased interconnectedness and interdependence among nations and cultures.
3. Inequality: The uneven distribution of income, wealth, or opportunities among individuals or groups within a society.
4. Nationalism: A political ideology that emphasizes loyalty, devotion, and support for one's nation, often to the exclusion or detriment of other nations or groups.
5. Neo-Luddism: A philosophy that opposes the introduction and advancement of new technologies, particularly those that are seen as threatening to existing jobs, skills, and ways of life.
6. Populism: A political approach that seeks to appeal to the interests, desires, and frustrations of the general public, often by presenting "the people" as a unified group in opposition to "the elite" or "the establishment."

7. Protectionism: The practice of shielding a country's domestic industries and producers from foreign competition through the use of tariffs, quotas, subsidies, or other restrictive trade policies.
8. Sabotage: The deliberate destruction, obstruction, or disruption of equipment, infrastructure, or systems, often as a form of protest, resistance, or retaliation.
9. Social Contract: The implicit agreement between individuals and their government or society, which outlines the rights, duties, and obligations of each party and forms the basis for the legitimacy of the social and political order.
10. Wealth Distribution: The manner in which wealth, assets, and resources are divided and allocated among individuals or groups within a society or economy.

Practical Applications:

1. Anticipate and prepare for potential social and political unrest: Businesses, governments, and individuals should be aware of the potential for increased social and political instability as a result of the disruptive effects of the Information Age. Developing contingency plans and strategies to mitigate the impact of such unrest on opera-

tions, investments, and personal well-being will be important.

2. Invest in education and training programs: To help individuals adapt to the changing demands of the cybereconomy, it will be crucial to invest in education and training programs that foster the development of new skills, knowledge, and competencies. This may involve promoting lifelong learning, reskilling initiatives, and access to online learning resources.

3. Develop inclusive policies and social protection measures: Governments and organizations should work to develop policies and social protection measures that help to mitigate the impact of technological disruption on individuals and communities. This may include exploring universal basic income schemes, portable benefits systems, or other forms of financial support and security.

4. Foster responsible innovation and technology governance: To address the potential negative consequences of technological change, it will be important to promote responsible innovation practices and effective technology governance frameworks. This may involve developing ethical guidelines for the development and

deployment of new technologies, ensuring transparency and accountability in the use of data and algorithms, and engaging in multi-stakeholder dialogues to address the social and economic implications of technological advancements.

5. Promote digital literacy and inclusion: Encouraging digital literacy and ensuring inclusive access to digital technologies and platforms will be essential in enabling individuals and communities to participate in and benefit from the Information Age. This may involve initiatives to bridge the digital divide, provide affordable Internet access, and support the development of digital skills and competencies.

6. Engage in proactive communication and stakeholder engagement: To build trust and foster a shared understanding of the benefits and challenges of technological change, businesses, governments, and other organizations should engage in proactive communication and stakeholder engagement efforts. This may involve developing clear and accessible narratives about the impact of technology on society, creating forums for open dialogue and collaboration, and working to address the concerns and aspirations of diverse stakeholder groups.

Chapter 6

The Twilight of Democracy

The Information Age will impact the future of democracy and political governance. The traditional model of representative democracy, which emerged in the context of the Industrial Age, may be increasingly ill-suited to the challenges and opportunities of the cybereconomy. The complexity and pace of change in the global economy and society may strain the capacity of traditional political institutions and processes to keep up with the demands of governance and decision-making.

However, there is potential for the Information Age to create new opportunities for more participatory and decentralized forms of democracy. The rise of digital technologies and networks could enable innovative forms of citizen engagement and collaboration, such as online deliberation and decision-making platforms, which could help to revitalize and transform democratic governance.

Nonetheless, the Information Age could pose significant risks to the stability and legitimacy of democratic institutions. The increasing concentration of wealth and power in the hands of a small number of tech giants and digital platforms could undermine the accountability and responsiveness of political systems, while the spread of misinformation and propaganda through social media could erode public trust and social cohesion.

To navigate these challenges, individuals and societies will need to rethink the foundations of democratic governance for the Information Age. This may involve developing new forms of political participation and representation that are better suited to the realities of the cybereconomy, as well as promoting digital literacy and critical thinking skills that can help citizens to navigate the complex and often confusing landscape of online information and discourse. Ultimately, the future of democracy in the Information Age will depend on the ability of individuals and societies to adapt and innovate in the face of rapid technological and social change.

Key Ideas:

- The traditional model of representative democracy may be increasingly ill-suited to the challenges and opportunities of the Information Age.
- The complexity and pace of change in the global economy and society may strain the

capacity of traditional political institutions and processes.

- The rise of digital technologies and networks could create new opportunities for more participatory and decentralized forms of democracy.
- The increasing concentration of wealth and power in the hands of tech giants and digital platforms could undermine the accountability and responsiveness of political systems.
- The spread of misinformation and propaganda through social media could erode public trust and social cohesion.
- Individuals and societies will need to rethink the foundations of democratic governance for the Information Age, developing new forms of political participation and representation and promoting digital literacy and critical thinking skills.

Vocabulary:

1. Cybereconomy: The economic system that emerges as a result of the widespread adoption of digital technologies and the Internet.

2. Participatory Democracy: A form of democracy in which citizens actively participate in the decision-making process, rather than simply electing representatives.
3. Decentralized Governance: A system of governance in which power and decision-making authority are distributed among a network of actors and institutions.
4. Digital Literacy: The ability to effectively navigate, evaluate, and create digital information and media, as well as to communicate and collaborate using digital tools and platforms.
5. Critical Thinking: The ability to analyze and evaluate information and arguments in a clear, rational, and reflective way, in order to make informed judgments and decisions.
6. Social Cohesion: The degree to which members of a society feel a sense of belonging, trust, and shared identity with one another, and are willing to cooperate and support each other in pursuit of common goals.

Practical Applications:

1. Experiment with new forms of political participation and representation, such as online deliberation and

decision-making platforms, to revitalize and transform democratic governance for the Information Age.

2. Invest in digital literacy and critical thinking education to help citizens navigate the complex landscape of online information and discourse.

3. Promote transparency and accountability in the tech industry to mitigate the risks of concentrated wealth and power in the hands of tech giants and digital platforms.

4. Foster a culture of empathy and understanding in online discourse to combat the spread of misinformation and propaganda and promote greater social cohesion and trust.

5. Explore alternative models of governance and decision-making, such as direct democracy and decentralized approaches, that are better suited to the realities of the cybereconomy.

Chapter 7

Morality and Crime in the "Natural Economy" of the Information Age

The Information Age will impact the nature of morality and crime in society. The rise of the cybereconomy and the increasing importance of digital assets and transactions may create new opportunities for criminal activity and moral hazard, while also challenging traditional notions of property rights and social norms.

The blurring of boundaries between the physical and digital worlds will be a key feature of the "natural economy" of the Information Age. This could create new challenges for law enforcement and regulatory authorities, as traditional methods of surveillance and control become less effective in the face of decentralized and anonymous digital networks.

Furthermore, the Information Age may create new opportunities for individuals and organizations to engage in criminal activities, such as hacking, cybertheft, and digital fraud. The increasing value and liquidity of digital assets, like cryptocurrencies and online reputation, could incentivize bad actors to exploit vulnerabilities and manipulate markets for personal gain.

There are potential implications of the Information Age for traditional notions of property rights and social norms. The rise of the sharing economy and the increasing importance of access over ownership could challenge the foundations of capitalist society. Additionally, the spread of digital surveillance and data mining could erode individual privacy and autonomy.

To navigate these challenges, individuals and societies will need to develop new frameworks for morality and justice in the Information Age. This may involve rethinking traditional notions of property rights and ownership, as well as developing new forms of digital governance and regulation to mitigate the risks of criminal activity and moral hazard in the cybereconomy.

Key Ideas:

- The rise of the cybereconomy may create new opportunities for criminal activity and moral hazard.
- The blurring of boundaries between the physical and digital worlds could challenge traditional methods of law enforcement and regulation.
- The increasing value of digital assets could

incentivize bad actors to exploit vulnerabilities and manipulate markets.
- The sharing economy and the importance of access over ownership could challenge the foundations of capitalist society.
- Digital surveillance and data mining could erode individual privacy and autonomy.
- New frameworks for morality and justice will be needed in the Information Age, including rethinking property rights and developing new forms of digital governance and regulation.

Vocabulary:

1. Cybereconomy: The economic system that emerges as a result of the widespread adoption of digital technologies and the Internet.
2. Moral Hazard: A situation in which an individual or organization is more likely to take risks or behave recklessly because they do not bear the full costs or consequences of their actions.
3. Cybertheft: The unauthorized access to or theft of digital assets, such as financial information, intellectual property, or personal data.

4. Digital Fraud: The use of digital technologies and networks to deceive or mislead others for personal gain, such as through phishing scams, fake websites, or online Ponzi schemes.
5. Sharing Economy: An economic model based on the sharing of access to goods and services, often through peer-to-peer digital platforms, rather than individual ownership.
6. Digital Governance: The use of digital technologies and data to support and enhance the processes of governance and decision-making, such as through online voting, public consultation, or algorithmic regulation.

Practical Applications:

1. Develop new frameworks for digital property rights and ownership to accommodate the unique characteristics of digital assets and transactions, such as shared equity or usage-based pricing.

2. Invest in cybersecurity and digital resilience to mitigate the risks of criminal activity and moral hazard in the cybereconomy.

. . .

3. Promote digital literacy and critical thinking skills to help individuals and organizations navigate the complex landscape of the cybereconomy.

4. Foster a culture of digital ethics and responsibility among individuals, organizations, and governments through codes of conduct and best practices for online behavior and transactions.

5. Explore new forms of digital governance and regulation, such as frameworks for the oversight and accountability of digital platforms and networks, and new approaches to online dispute resolution and restorative justice.

Chapter 8

The Commercialization of Sovereignty

The nature of sovereignty and the role of the state in society will shift in the Information Age. The rise of the cybereconomy and the increasing importance of digital assets and transactions may lead to a fundamental shift in the way sovereignty is conceptualized and exercised, with far-reaching implications for the future of governance and social organization.

One of the key features of the Information Age will be the "commercialization of sovereignty," as the traditional functions of the state are increasingly taken over by private actors and market forces. The increasing complexity and pace of change in the global economy, coupled with the declining effectiveness of traditional forms of regulation and control, may lead to a situation in which the state is no longer able to provide the public goods and services that are essential for social stability and prosperity.

Instead, a future is envisioned in which sovereignty is

effectively "unbundled" and sold off to the highest bidder, with different aspects of governance and social organization being provided by a range of private actors and institutions. This could lead to the emergence of new forms of "private cities" and "charter states," in which individuals and communities are able to choose the systems of governance and social organization that best suit their needs and preferences.

However, the commercialization of sovereignty could also pose significant risks and challenges for social stability and cohesion. The increasing fragmentation and privatization of governance could lead to a situation in which the basic needs and rights of citizens are no longer guaranteed by the state, leading to greater inequality and social polarization.

To navigate these challenges, individuals and societies will need to rethink the fundamental principles of governance and social organization for the Information Age. This may involve developing new forms of public-private partnerships and collaborative governance, as well as exploring alternative models of citizenship and social welfare that are better suited to the realities of the cybereconomy.

Key Ideas:

- The rise of the cybereconomy may lead to a fundamental shift in the way sovereignty is conceptualized and exercised.

- The increasing complexity and pace of change in the global economy, coupled with the declining effectiveness of traditional forms of regulation, may lead to a situation in which the state is no longer able to provide essential public goods and services.
- The commercialization of sovereignty could lead to the emergence of new forms of "private cities" and "charter states," where individuals and communities choose the systems of governance that best suit their needs.
- The increasing fragmentation and privatization of governance could pose significant risks for social stability and cohesion, leading to greater inequality and polarization.
- Navigating these challenges will require rethinking the fundamental principles of governance and social organization for the Information Age, developing new forms of public-private partnerships, collaborative governance, and alternative models of citizenship and social welfare.

Vocabulary:

1. Unbundling: The process of separating the different components or functions of a product or service, allowing them to be provided by different actors or institutions.
2. Private Cities: Urban areas that are developed and governed by private actors or institutions, rather than by traditional public authorities.
3. Charter States: Political entities that are established through a charter or contract between a group of individuals or communities, rather than through traditional forms of state formation or conquest.
4. Public-Private Partnerships: Collaborative arrangements between public and private actors or institutions, designed to leverage the strengths and resources of both sectors in pursuit of common goals or objectives.
5. Collaborative Governance: A model of governance that emphasizes the importance of collaboration, negotiation, and shared decision-making among a range of stakeholders, rather than top-down control by a central authority.

Practical Applications:

1. Explore new models of public-private partnerships and collaborative governance that can leverage the

strengths and resources of both sectors in pursuit of common goals and objectives.

2. Develop alternative models of citizenship and social welfare that are better suited to the realities of the cybereconomy, such as universal basic income or social credit systems.

3. Foster a culture of digital citizenship and civic engagement among individuals and communities by promoting digital literacy, critical thinking skills, and participation in online decision-making processes.

4. Promote greater transparency and accountability in the governance of private actors and institutions through new frameworks for regulation and oversight, as well as greater public scrutiny and engagement.

5. Explore new forms of global governance and cooperation, such as frameworks for the coordination and harmonization of national and regional policies and regulations, and greater dialogue and collaboration among global stakeholders.

Chapter 9

The Fate of The Nation-State

The nation-state will become the dominant form of political organization in the modern world. The rise of the cybereconomy and the increasing importance of digital assets and transactions may pose significant challenges to the traditional functions and legitimacy of the nation-state, with far-reaching implications for the future of governance and social organization.

One of the key features of the Information Age will be the increasing "deterritorialization" of economic and social activity, as more and more interactions and transactions take place in the virtual realm of cyberspace. This could undermine the ability of nation-states to control and regulate economic activity within their borders, as well as to provide the public goods and services that are essential for social stability and prosperity.

At the same time, the increasing complexity and interdependence of the global economy may also challenge the ability of nation-states to effectively manage and respond to the challenges of the Information Age. The traditional tools of national policy and regulation may be increasingly ineffective in the face of global economic and technological forces, leading to a situation in which nation-states are increasingly "hollowed out" and unable to fulfill their basic functions.

The chapter also explores the potential implications of the Information Age for the future of national identity and social cohesion. The increasing fragmentation and individualization of society, coupled with the rise of new forms of digital communities and networks, could undermine the ability of nation-states to provide a sense of shared purpose and belonging for their citizens.

To navigate these challenges, individuals and societies will need to rethink the fundamental principles of governance and social organization for the Information Age. This may involve exploring new forms of global governance and cooperation, as well as developing alternative models of citizenship and social welfare that are better suited to the realities of the cybereconomy.

Key Ideas:

- The rise of the cybereconomy may pose significant challenges to the traditional functions and legitimacy of the nation-state.
- The increasing "deterritorialization" of economic and social activity could undermine

the ability of nation-states to control and regulate economic activity within their borders and provide essential public goods and services.

- The increasing complexity and interdependence of the global economy may challenge the ability of nation-states to effectively manage and respond to the challenges of the Information Age, leading to a "hollowing out" of their basic functions.
- The increasing fragmentation and individualization of society, coupled with the rise of new digital communities and networks, could undermine the ability of nation-states to provide a sense of shared purpose and belonging for their citizens.
- Navigating these challenges will require rethinking the fundamental principles of governance and social organization for the Information Age, exploring new forms of global governance and cooperation, and developing alternative models of citizenship and social welfare.

Vocabulary:

1. Deterritorialization: The process by which economic and social activities become

increasingly detached from specific geographic locations or territories.

2. Hollowing Out: The process by which the traditional functions and capacities of an institution or organization are gradually eroded or undermined, often as a result of external pressures or challenges.
3. Digital Communities: Online groups or networks of individuals who share common interests, values, or identities, and who interact and communicate primarily through digital technologies and platforms.
4. Global Governance: The system of rules, norms, and institutions that govern the behavior of states and other actors in the international system, often with the goal of promoting cooperation and addressing common challenges.
5. Alternative Citizenship: Models of citizenship and social belonging that are not based on traditional notions of national identity or territorial attachment, but rather on shared values, interests, or experiences.

Practical Applications:

1. Develop new frameworks for global governance and cooperation that can promote greater coordination

and harmonization of policies and regulations across national borders.

2. Explore alternative models of citizenship and social welfare that are better suited to the realities of the Information Age, such as new forms of social safety nets and support systems that are not tied to traditional notions of national citizenship or territorial attachment.

3. Foster a culture of digital citizenship and civic engagement among individuals and communities by promoting digital literacy, critical thinking skills, and participation in online decision-making processes.

4. Invest in the development of new forms of public goods and services that are better suited to the realities of the Information Age, such as exploring new models of public-private partnerships and collaborative governance.

5. Promote greater understanding and dialogue across cultures and communities through new forms of intercultural education and exchange programs, as well as promoting empathy and respect for diversity in online and offline interactions.

Chapter 10

The Emergence of Private Law

The future of law and legal systems is expected to be fundamentally different from anything we've known before. The rise of the cybereconomy and the increasing importance of digital assets and transactions may lead to the emergence of new forms of private law and dispute resolution, with far-reaching implications for the future of governance and social organization.

One of the key features of the Information Age will be the increasing "privatization" of law and legal systems, as the traditional functions of the state in providing and enforcing legal rules and norms are increasingly taken over by private actors and institutions. The increasing complexity and specialization of the global economy, coupled with the declining effectiveness of traditional forms of legal regulation and enforcement, may lead to a situation in which the state is no longer able to provide the legal infrastructure and services that are essential for social stability and prosperity.

Instead, a future is envisioned in which law and legal systems are effectively "unbundled" and provided by a range of private actors and institutions, such as private arbitration and mediation services, online dispute resolution platforms, and blockchain-based smart contracts. This could lead to the emergence of new forms of "polycentric" legal systems, in which individuals and communities are able to choose the legal rules and norms that best suit their needs and preferences.

However, the emergence of private law and legal systems could also pose significant risks and challenges for social justice and the rule of law. The increasing fragmentation and privatization of legal systems could lead to a situation in which access to justice and legal remedies is increasingly determined by one's ability to pay, leading to greater inequality and social polarization.

To navigate these challenges, individuals and societies will need to rethink the fundamental principles of law and justice for the Information Age. This may involve developing new forms of public-private partnerships and collaborative governance in the provision of legal services, as well as exploring alternative models of legal education and training that are better suited to the realities of the cybereconomy.

Key Ideas:

- The rise of the cybereconomy may lead to the emergence of new forms of private law and dispute resolution.
- The increasing complexity of the global economy and the declining effectiveness of traditional legal regulation may lead to the state no longer being able to provide essential legal infrastructure and services.
- The emergence of private law and legal systems could lead to the development of new "polycentric" legal systems, where individuals and communities can choose the legal rules and norms that best suit their needs.
- The increasing fragmentation and privatization of legal systems could pose significant risks for social justice and the rule of law, leading to greater inequality and polarization.
- Navigating these challenges will require rethinking the fundamental principles of law and justice for the Information Age, developing new public-private partnerships in legal services, and exploring alternative models of legal education and training.

Vocabulary:

1. Privatization of Law: The process by which the traditional functions of the state in providing and enforcing legal rules and norms are increasingly taken over by private actors and institutions.
2. Polycentric Law: A system of law and legal governance in which multiple overlapping and competing jurisdictions and legal systems coexist and interact, often with the ability of individuals and communities to choose the legal rules and norms that apply to them.
3. Smart Contracts: Self-executing digital contracts with the terms of the agreement directly written into code, which automatically enforce the obligations of all parties involved.
4. Collaborative Governance: A model of governance that emphasizes the importance of collaboration, negotiation, and shared decision-making among a range of stakeholders, rather than top-down control by a central authority.
5. Alternative Legal Education: Models of legal education and training that are not based on traditional notions of legal professionalism or institutional certification, but rather on the acquisition of practical skills and knowledge relevant to the realities of the cybereconomy.

. . .

Practical Applications:

1. Develop new frameworks for the regulation and oversight of private legal systems to mitigate the risks of the privatization of law and promote transparency and accountability.

2. Explore new models of public-private partnerships in the provision of legal services to ensure greater access to justice and legal remedies in the face of the privatization of law.

3. Foster a culture of legal empowerment and self-help among individuals and communities to promote greater social justice and the rule of law in the face of the privatization of legal systems.

4. Invest in the development of new forms of legal education and training to ensure a supply of legal professionals and experts who are equipped to navigate the challenges of the Information Age.

5. Promote greater dialogue and cooperation among legal systems and jurisdictions to navigate the challenges of the

increasing fragmentation and polycentricity of legal systems, such as developing frameworks for the mutual recognition and enforcement of legal rules and decisions across jurisdictional boundaries.

Chapter 11

The Sovereign Individual and the Future of Morality

In the final chapter, the implications of the rise of the Sovereign Individual for the future of governance and social organization are explored. The Information Age will give rise to a new era of individual empowerment and self-governance, in which individuals will be free to choose their own communities, values, and ways of life. However, this transformation will also entail challenges and uncertainties, and guidance is offered on how individuals can navigate this new landscape and thrive in the age of the Sovereign Individual.

The emergence of the "Sovereign Individual" as the primary unit of social and economic organization will pose significant challenges and risks for social cohesion and stability, as traditional forms of social and political authority are eroded. To navigate these challenges, individuals and societies will need to develop new forms of governance and social organization that are better suited to the realities of the Information Age, including more decentralized and polycentric models of governance.

The rise of the Sovereign Individual will require a new kind of social contract, in which individuals take greater responsibility for their own welfare and security, while also recognizing the importance of social cooperation and mutual aid in the face of common challenges and risks. The future of governance in the Information Age will be shaped by the choices and actions of individuals, as they navigate the opportunities and challenges of the cybereconomy and assert their autonomy and independence in the face of changing social and political realities.

Key Ideas:

- The Information Age will lead to a greater diversity of moral and ethical frameworks, as individuals gain the ability to choose their own values and communities.
- The decline of the nation-state and the rise of the Sovereign Individual will lead to a shift away from universal moral codes towards more personalized and contextual approaches to ethics.
- The future of morality will be shaped by the ongoing negotiation and evolution of social norms within and between communities,

rather than by top-down imposition by political authorities.

- The rise of the Sovereign Individual will require a new kind of social contract, in which individuals take greater responsibility for their own welfare and security, while also recognizing the importance of social cooperation and mutual aid.
- The future of governance in the Information Age will be shaped by the choices and actions of individuals, as they navigate the opportunities and challenges of the cybereconomy and assert their autonomy and independence.

Vocabulary:

1. Moral Pluralism: The view that there are multiple, competing moral frameworks and values, rather than a single, universal set of moral truths.
2. Moral Entrepreneurship: The practice of actively shaping and promoting new moral norms and values, often in response to changing social and technological conditions.
3. Reputation Markets: Systems for tracking and evaluating the trustworthiness and reliability of individuals and organizations

based on their past behavior and performance.

4. Decentralized Governance: A model of governance in which decision-making power and authority are distributed among multiple actors and institutions, rather than being concentrated in a single centralized authority.
5. Polycentric Governance: A system of governance in which multiple overlapping and competing jurisdictions and authorities coexist and interact, often with the ability of individuals and communities to choose the governance arrangements that apply to them.
6. Social Contract: The implicit agreement between individuals and society regarding their rights and responsibilities towards one another, which forms the basis for legitimate political authority and social cooperation.
7. Mutual Aid: The practice of voluntary reciprocal exchange of resources and services for mutual benefit, often within a community or social network.
8. Individual Sovereignty: The idea that individuals have the ultimate authority and responsibility for governing their own lives and making decisions about their own welfare and security, free from external coercion or control.

. . .

Practical Applications:

1. Develop a strong sense of personal ethics and values, while remaining open to learning from and engaging with other moral perspectives.

2. Be prepared to navigate a world of increasing moral and cultural diversity, developing the skills of empathy, communication, and cross-cultural understanding.

3. Cultivate a reputation for integrity and trustworthiness, as this will become increasingly important in a world where reputation markets play a key role in social and economic interactions.

4. Engage in moral entrepreneurship where appropriate, working to shape and promote new moral norms and values that are better suited to the realities of the Information Age.

5. Foster a culture of individual responsibility and initiative, promoting greater self-reliance and entrepreneurship, and encouraging individuals to take an active role in shaping the governance arrangements that affect their lives.

. . .

6. Develop new models of decentralized and polycentric governance that are better suited to the realities of the Information Age, experimenting with new forms of community-based governance and exploring the potential of blockchain and other distributed ledger technologies.

7. Cultivate a sense of social solidarity and mutual aid among individuals and communities, developing new forms of social safety nets and support systems, and promoting greater empathy and understanding across different social and cultural groups.

8. Invest in the development of new forms of digital infrastructure and services, exploring new models of digital identity and reputation management, and promoting greater interoperability and standardization across different digital platforms and systems.

9. Promote greater dialogue and cooperation among different governance systems and models, developing new frameworks for the mutual recognition and exchange of ideas and best practices across different jurisdictions and communities, and promoting greater global coordination and collaboration in the face of common challenges and risks.

Chapter 12

Conclusion

"The Sovereign Individual" offers a thought-provoking and challenging vision of the future, one in which the traditional institutions and frameworks of the Industrial Age give way to a new era of individual empowerment and decentralized, market-driven social organization. By understanding the key ideas, vocabulary, and practical implications outlined in this study guide, readers can begin to proactively prepare themselves for the profound changes ahead, positioning themselves to thrive in a world where the power of the individual is increasingly paramount.

As the authors make clear, the transition to the Information Age will not be without its challenges and disruptions, as long-standing institutions and ways of life are upended and transformed. The rise of the Sovereign Individual may also bring with it new risks and downsides, such as increased inequality, social fragmentation, and the erosion of traditional safety nets. However, by acknowledging and preparing for these challenges, and by actively seeking out and engaging with like-minded individuals and communities, readers can help to shape a future that is more balanced, resilient, and equitable.

Ultimately, the path to personal sovereignty in the Information Age will require a combination of individual initiative, collective collaboration, and a willingness to embrace change and uncertainty. By cultivating the skills, knowledge, and mindset needed to succeed in this new era, and by taking concrete steps to prepare for the challenges and opportunities ahead, readers of The Sovereign Individual can play a vital role in creating a world that is more free, more just, and more abundant than ever before.

So let this be a call to action: to take the first steps towards personal sovereignty, to seek out and engage with the communities and technologies that will shape the future, and to embrace the challenges and opportunities of the Information Age with courage, curiosity, and determination. The future belongs to those who are willing to seize it - and with the insights and tools provided in this book, the path forward has never been clearer.

About the Author

Hugo Rowley attended the University of Edinburgh and worked in fund management before starting Learner's Permit Guides. He loves learning new things but found there weren't enough hours in the day to learn as much as he wanted. He created these guides to help other people who are curious and want to keep learning.

Hugo lives in LA and Malta with his family. He enjoys exploring new places and ideas with them.

www.ingramcontent.com/pod-product-compliance
Ingram Content Group UK Ltd.
Pitfield, Milton Keynes, MK11 3LW, UK
UKHW040011200726
13854UKWH00001B/155

9 798224 329380